The Dead Queen of Bohemia

The Dead Queen
of Bohemia

New & Collected Poems

Jenni Fagan

Polygon

First published in Great Britain in 2016 by
Polygon, an imprint of Birlinn Limited

Birlinn Limited
West Newington House
10 Newington Road
Edinburgh
EH9 1QS

www.polygonbooks.co.uk

ISBN 978 1 84697 339 0
eBook ISBN 978 0 85790 898 8

British Library Cataloguing-in-Publication Data
A catalogue record for this book is available from the British Library.

Typeset by Koinonia, Manchester
Printed and bound by TJ International, Padstow, Cornwall

for Boo

Contents

Collection I: *New Poems*

Collection II: *The Dead Queen of Bohemia*
(*first published in 2010*)

Collection III: *Urchin Belle*
(*first published in 2009*)

Collection I
New Poems

I Wanna Be Your Dog

My son and I
have a dog called Hank
who
one of us
wanted to call Fluffy
but the other
refused to spend ten years in parks
shouting
Fluffy!
unless —
the dog was a Rottweiler,
or a Pit bull.

Hank is just an imprint
of light
in our idle conversations.

Sometimes we see a dog
in the street
and I ask him,
is that what Hank looks like?
It never is
and we like him just like this,

our endless Hank,
a piston on the beach,

jaws snapping at one wave after another
or laid out under my feet
while I read poetry
to strangers
who are no stranger than I —
except for that one
up the back,

and also the woman I meet in the loos
who sings me a song;
then tells me
her dog
overdosed on paint fumes,
and the stain (where he laid tripping
in his last hours)
is still on her carpet.

I don't ask her why
she let her dog get high on paint fumes.

Or, why she didn't open a window.

She tells me about a cult;
she's trying to escape
but they keep peering through her letter box,
shouting
we know
you're in there!

She says she didn't realise they were a cult
thought they were just friendly people,
and she was lonely
and had nobody to talk to about Jesus,
or her dead dog
who asphyxiated
watched over by floral vases,
while saints
wept
      the
          hours
               away.

She was walking home from Norwich market
when she finally realised,
by then she'd given them her money
and dignity,
she'd been lured
and indoctrinated
she said she had to leave
the country
immediately
— to avoid further brainwashing.

I didn't let her know the brainwashers
have Fiddle-Dee and Fiddle-Dum
in every port and customs
to make sure
those with clear sight
don't get through
unseen.

She wasn't really
listening to me read poetry
and we were not in an echoey
toilet with a dripping
cistern . . .

We were on the phone
for the seventeenth time,
because we were trying to swap flats
or I was trying to swap flats
and she was trying to make friends.

She asked if my housing association
would mind
if she had
— seven parrots
— two cats
— a rat
— a budgie
and maybe (if she got over her heartbreak)
another dog.

I said *no*,
I was sure that would be fine
because I would have said anything — at that point
to get
      out
         of
            Edinburgh.

In the end I didn't swap houses with crazy-cult-lady
and she's probably still in the cult
calling strangers,
telling them about her dead dog
even to this day.

Instead, I swapped
flats with a woman in Peckham
who, when I visited to look at her place
had a stack of boxes
in the corner
covered with sheets
and from that part of the room
there was an endless scratching
and I had the idea
of tiny hearts
and lungs beating.

She told me about the council tax band
and the chinese neighbours
and the man out back whose wife threw him out once a month
who was 78
who would spend all day
shouting:
Jean! Jean! Let me back in,
I fought in the war for this country,
let me back into the house, Jean!
I didn't kiss her, Jean!
I didn't, let me in!

But Jean would not let him back in
until he'd been out there
for eight hours
and this would happen every three weeks,
all the neighbours would hear it
with our windows
flung wide
open
     to
        summer —

where trees would rustle —
where trees would shake their boughs
to get passers by attention.

Where I would later photograph the harvest moon
in Peckham park
at midnight
and it would turn into a dragon
and I would write a note —
on the back of the photograph
to a writer I admired
saying I wanted to send her a moon
that had turned

into a dragon
and wasn't it the way of things — moons liked to do that sometimes.

All the while
this woman is talking
and some kind of thing is scratching
and I imagine
what might be under
this huge stack of boxes,
and thin paint-stained sheets.
So, I ask her
what's in there?
and she tells me
it's depressed rats,
she yanks the cover off nine crates stacked up to the roof
each filled with rats,
— *they're depressed,* she says,
NO FUCKING SHIT! I think.

I rescue depressed rats, she says.

I nod like I understand
and wonder if I can set a few of those rats free
when she's not looking.

She looks different now she's showed me the rats
now I know she is the pied piper
of verminous Prozac
playing her
whistle
so rats can smile
again, and can feel connected
to themselves
and each other
and even begin to brush their teeth once more —
think about starting over!

6

Depressed-rat-lady,
is the one I actually swap flats with and she takes her rats
to live in a room I painted,
in a council estate
block-of-six
where a woman runs around the building
half naked
until police
take her away,
it happens most days,
and every weekend.

So when I'm out walking
with my son
we often see a Hank,
and I imagine him
sharing our life,
our love
I think of a day when Hank
will come with me to readings
or rodeos
or renaissance fairs
and my son says Hank will be a good
friend for our cats,
Milky and Star
who too,
are not
real yet,
because we're in a rental
with a hostile landlord
who doesn't like cats.

I'm trying to buy something
but nothing is cheap
and a man called Yassar
keeps snapping up everything,
his purse
is bigger
than my brain,

It's a conundrum
a logistical puzzle
of how to get somewhere to live
where we can get this dog
and these cats,
I think about it every day.

And when my son and I walk along the river
throwing sticks
looking for the heron
in the highest boughs,
I always tell him *yes, yes, yes* —
it's definite.

We will get our Hank one day.

Back in the Caravan (or the Wolf & the Minstrel)

Sometimes I think
the poetry will leave

me — who it came to at seven
scrawled in stolen

notebooks, the whole world
colder than a tin room

nightmares so real
I peed in the corner,

shapes and shadows
unfamiliar as a hall,

I slept on the floor
climbed into some bed

in the morning
like I'd had it in me

to dream there —
I often shrank to a dot.

There were accents,
people in dressing gowns or tracksuits

they'd go places and come back,
they had their likes and dislikes

there was dust
on porcelain cats

soft meat, mushed potatoes
a thud of plates on tables

awkward chairs
patternous child-eating floors —

my voice left altogether
who could blame it.

I scribbled on the page
one word followed another —

look at that!

Sometimes I think
the poetry will leave

me — who it sat with at dawn
in the high-rise

after the long night,
when he brought a red bulb,

it still came to
tweak a smile

it watched over
a pre-teen suicide

wholly willing to die —
anyone's right,

it was the red and blue
of disco lights,

metal braces grinding
crooked teeth

it was the zap-light
on tube-lines, flashes of rats

running along tracks
the heart drum —

a merry-go-nowhere
it knew skeletons

wear confused people
who get locked up,

locked out, locked in,
it was inevitable as lust

karaoke was no cure
Sudoku posed no challenge

it knew the smell of sea
in my knickers after I bathed

in the river each day
when I slept in the forest

for a week (not even a teen)
it arrived (then) as a lullaby

precise as a child.

It refused to leave
it vowed to always argue

the point, it said the shallow
breath is never endless,

it repainted skies indiscriminately,
laid down each night

to listen to my heart,
promised to remain uncomatose

if I did, stacked up seconds
in corners taught me

to knuckle my tombstones
under Doc boots —

it always turned the music up!
It knew the wolf & the minstrel,

married me without letting me know,
it went to the other side

and nailed up a picture
of us betrothed.

I Swam in Blue

I never did like radishes
of any sort — on cold days
I swam in blue.

Poem After Listening to Neruda

What we want, it so happens — we are.

I am sick — a waterproof swan,
staring into the wombs of horses
I am the still wool,
I am the elevator's spectacles.

You — are how nature is separated.

And it so happens — I am sick,
and you are fingernails, hair and shadow,
on the stair (where he killed a man
with a balloon in his ear)

my green knife!

Every day a wounded wheel,
television reflected
in my windows,
expected but no less hideous!

A giant hand — so marvellous.

Venom *is* umbilical,
bye, bye grandma —
under the house,
buzzing gas again.

Send out a kite, a kite to catch.

It will fly by your window,
go on — look out
now,
it won't destroy you.

Forget everything!

The park-light (is gold)
and the people
are beginning to point,
the sky is opening.

Look out now, it won't destroy you!

Cold as a Girl

Icicles
like
narwhal
tusks,
or the gnarled
bony
finger
of winter
herself.

Instruction Manual for Suicidal Girls
(Boys, Trolls & Troglodytes)

You have all rights to muse
on methods

modes,
transport

last meals, last fucks, first leap,
loose knot

suitcase and vicoden
but here's some advice

from a girl who travelled to the other side
(age 12)

most people do not get it right,
& the other side

has an intensity so unbearable
it makes the madness of worldlings

sound like a lullaby
you'll never sing again.

And if you are 12 you will be preoccupied
as your organs fail

with why you never drove an ice-cream truck
or if they know you are a virgin

when they embalm
and deliver

& how you never owned a ranch
or two wolves

or saw a year
of full moons,

or a grandchild who looks in your eyes
and sees there that —

time,
is what we travel

only to find
in the worst minutes

that we live
many lives

in this,
one life.

In being
we find ways

to be.

Tic-Tac-Toe

tic
tac
toe
two
for
me
three
for
the
next
world,
four
for
angina
twelve
for
migraine
tic
tac
tum
scratching
my
throat
now
swelling
up
my
gullet
now
swallowing
like
a
pelican
swigging

'em down
with
malibu
tim
tee
hoo
just
another
few.

I Had Been Excited
to Hear a Blue Light from the Inside

Movement —
people in white.

Humming machines
lament my return.

My father is holding my thumb,
he is not my father but I won't tell him

his mouth says things
as I go.

The dark
won't dance.

People rush.
The lights don't lie.

Bleep.

    Bleeep.

        Bleeeee . . .

Lie Down

Here in the grass.

Where's the place I live?

It's somewhere near.

All the streets look the same.

Is it where they propped you up, rang the bell, then ran away?

It wasn't that door.

Why do you only sleep in purest black?

They raised me as a bat.

Where are your fangs?

Under these braces.

What was the street called then?

I didn't write it down . . .

Move your hand away, just let me do it.

How will I get back?

I don't know.

Six Hours to Sunrise

The midnight swish,
laughter as polis
scrabbled down the viaduct,
the short breath

and the soft moan
are aw gone
and they lie
in hooses wi doors.

Ma fists clenched,
knees up tae ma chin
arse damp wi moss stains
breath sour, I stay

inside ma hoody
where trees cannae see,
the viaduct bridge
heavy on concrete haunches

metal forearms graffiti'd,
bolted elbows an' bracelets
ay ivy trail down tae
rusty train tracks

littered wi lager cans
flat tyres, shopping trolleys
an auld suitcase ripped
apart an' stinking ay pish.

Thirteen

We were at Pontins or Butlins
or some shite,

clubhouse
flickered down the road,

adults sipping flourescent
cocktails

shards of laughter,
hi-de-hi performers,

we were out back,
the kids' disco

empty except for two blue
lights bopping

on a dance floor,
someone lit a joint,

a guy ran his fingers
down your spine

a small audience
of boys rapt

(as I was)
by you.

Wicked Willy

Three little boys, where should they be?
White hands clutch black widows,[1]
crouching under tables,
peeping up the kilts

swimming in the Ellies Hole
of every town
mocking superheroes
they really wish tae be.

Three little boys, where should they be?
Not where these old eyes
can see the tragedy
of future days unfold

like the wings
of the Gargoyle swooping
wearing one red eye
& a terrible smile.

First little boy
hangs spread eagled —
curly hair snot nose
paper skin & china bones

as the whirly-gig[2] spins.
little paper-cut-doll
kens his crime
was the worst ay them all.

[1] Black widows — a kind of catapult.
[2] Whirly-gig — round clothes line.

Pale-face bug-eye Jesus
stealing pity
like golden eggs,
sucking 'em dry

he places them back
so gently! Two little generals.
march around him,
ruling an army

of condemnation.
risen high on the shoulders
of mass hysteria,
swing him

swing him
swing him on the line
fist tae jaw,
bloodier each time.

Two little gods,
wearing swastika smiles
inform the one way trip to hell
will be an infinity

in arriving he will greet it
with relief pale-face
bug-eye Jesus
the golden egg thief.

Our Last Card

My beloved
and I lie in a bath

two junkied
queens on a card,

in a safe house,
while the guns are out

and a million other under-agers
tout wares on streets

that despoil them,
we trade five hundred

bloody little deaths
between us,

deal them out
to each other like cards,

until one of us says
snap.

Unrequited

In your bed,
(my foot by your foot)

I do not care
if a volcano from Iceland

brings forth a 75,000 year ice-age
or if meteors rain,

or if the walls are paper
blowing in the wind,

I have no fear,
(my toe touching your toe)

of even
the last breath.

Daffodils

You walked me to rehearsal,
no one was out

the streets were ours,
every stone in the wall

my fingers traced
made me want you

more —
our come-down

could not compete
with love

you picked me
daffodils in the park,

my rehearsal
room that morning,

(a grotty concrete
bunker with no windows

glitter on the walls)
was bursts of yellow,

me switching on a kettle,
coffee, cigarettes

the band tuning up
seven more hours of loud-quiet, loud-quiet

before you could touch me again.

Pretty Girls Dig Graves

I'm in the job centre
telling the woman,

I'm sick of cleaning
or serving

or typing
or shit-n-fucking-schizzle,

I want to go for the gravedigger job.

The security man
escorts a girl

out who's just headbutted
the plastic screen.

I used to chop wood,
I was lethal on monkey bars

my arms can take
the heft ay a spade.

She types something
on the screen

while I think of blue skies
and square views

iPod on, working outside.
Put me forward!

She won't even look at me.
She stamps my book.

I never even get an interview.

The Writer is Present

In your eye
a tiny window,

in each square
there is light

we are open, like the mouths
of fishes

in a time
of great separation,

sixteen others
in a room silent and dense

just looking
at another person.

We go years
without doing this!

You are every lover
I am glad to have lain with.

We are present.
I will remember this.

The Man Was Not the Man

Deathwatch beetles ticked in the roof of a barn
I typed in

it wasn't a barn,
it was just built like one,
the man had said something —

he said he didn't say it. It was going to be like that.

He'd researched me before we met.
I had a rabbit for a heart,
and no halo.

He fixed one pretty and too tight right around my neck.

Trying to grab
a phone while
flying along a hallway

I think it landed in the bath. *Go to your room*, he said.

I wasn't anywhere near free
I didn't know the route
to Tipperary

I played a whistle, tapped my foot gently.

My soul walked out
I'm not staying for this shit,
she spat and sashayed out the door,

I found her perched at the top of a dying oak tree.

Put a ladder against
the trunk
but it wasn't tall enough

I got a bow and arrow and took aim.

You can't shoot a soul,
dickhead, she says.
Loneliness without her

a hole in my heart where a beat should be.

It's summer, it's London,
scratches on the bath
my huge sculpture of a Scold's Bridle on the grass.

I reach for the saw.

It's a buzz-cut into the trunk
that soul is so high!
She needs to come back,

There's silence in the bathroom —

it's still London
a summer of trips in pyjamas for gin,
flip-flops and circular walks.

Where is the golden heart and the artist?

Where is the man?
This one shoots an arrow in my heart
over supper every night.

I am too weary for words or phone calls.

Instead, I saw until it burns.
Realise too late
the trunk will fall through three gardens

and if it hits a person they'll be dead.

The crack and crash is so loud
I run across the lawn,
leap through the window

lie on the floor, heart battering

outside a row
of garden fences
gammy as broken teeth

and me trying to find a tree feller

in South East London,
to saw up a huge
sick old oak

before the neighbours get back

outside
the garden
is dappled in sun,

for the first time

since I moved here
there is warmth
on my skin.

He Was an Actor (18) He Liked to Listen to the Theatre Breathe

What happened to long-haired boys
with full lips

and gentle hands
that would stroke my hair

at 5 a.m.,
sit on my doorstep

all night
while I slept,

and later that month
a letter would arrive

sealed by wax
with two black roses.

Exit Stage Left, Admitting the Abyss

Fists fly in a bar of fallen angels
with quicksilver eyes and mercury tongues,

pint glasses smash over two guys,
boss jumps on someone's head in the road,

a French girl: *is it always like this to work here?*
I tell her she might be *better off in a call centre or something,*

ashtray flies across a room to notify last orders,
two shots of every white spirit

and a barman trussed up in the cellar,
a sports bag full of unmarked notes,

paranoid tribes at the door past 4 a.m. trying to score,
the long white line and never knowing what was at the end of it,

doing a Sunday morning shift after a night
where tomorrow seemed unlikely

yet there I was — Mercury Rev sounding like demonic
satanistic, imp kind of creatures

and Tall Schmink can still speak so he has to pour pints
'cos I can't communicate any more

just roll cigarettes and keep breathing, think
about how there used to be an emergency button

under the beer taps, it would be pressed
to indicate the presence of sawn-off shotguns

a wee red light and buzzer wired up to the cellar
so the old boss could scramble up a keg hatch,

and getaway by bicycle.

The Fall of Then

I got broke
it was an ugly truth
bloody
messy

all pervasive
soul decay
breathe it in deep
hyperventilate

sit up a tree
disappearing
those leaves must fall
it's mulch

that feeds the soil.
It's all good
so get grateful
I took the kind of kick-in

that fells empires
I am not felled
limping,
bloody, messy

kind of perfect really,
can't believe this skin
contained it all
so long.

The Secret Seal Wife

I left my skin by the shore,
went to swim
in my real form,

the lorries
were leaving
for France,

you were fast asleep
while I floated
on the lake,

later I showered
away brine
that hint of silver —

put my human skin
back on so
you wouldn't know

I never show you,
I know
how much men

(like you)
value the ability
to skin a pelt.

Vertebrae & Friends

My bones are not from here.
My bones know.

The Narcissist & the Light Stasher

They did not like
sunlight on your skin,

ordered you sit in the shade,
said: *you are repellent*

vile, they kept you pale,
insistent endless bullshit

made you wonder
if it was in fact true

the fault was yours?
Clever like that, they are.

Still, the moon
shines for you regardless

all the brighter in fact
child, you stash

light in your cells
wherever you find it

eyes like a magpie
trained to catch a glitter

on water,
reflections bright

on buildings
the long ocean glade

or shushing fields of gold,
so when the dark

falls (and it does)
after all this time

it's die
or glow.

When I Say Shoe, I Mean Converse
(Old and Tattered As)

I always have
one Converse
in a cupboard
pointing to home.

I don't leave it like that
it turns itself
in the night
I ignore it each morning.

Kintsugi

Japanese
believe —
what's broken,
is more beautiful
for
the cracks,
which
is
why
they
fill them
with gold.

The Rocks, the Crags & the Sun-Worm

There are things
you will never see
in me,
places I have understood
in welly boots,
the bare rock
and it's ancestral stare
warriors in Woolworths,
fire-bombs
through letterboxes,
debris,
spires of smoke,
rising through rain.

New Poem

Your mum thought I was a weirdo
something to pity,

she mistrusted
why I would not covet

Fruit or Loom,
nor two-stripes,

or a high-street
that could only be sailed

tolerably
on Elless and Dee —

every lunch-time,
the school bell:

I'd sit on your front step,
your neighbours tweaking the curtains

watching-the-wierdo-watching-it-stare-the-other-way.
a chain-smoking wolf-cub

who slept-in-the-woods
half lichen

half echo
spitting down

the long black well,
while you asked me to love you

dressed me in your brother's
football top,

you wore your mother's spectacles
played tic-tac-toe

with tablets
we both knew

would bury us,
and one day they'd impale

our heads on the gates
of the city

so we could smile
at the children

who came there to fly.

It Would Have Been the Actions of an Insane Woman, but I Know the Thought of It Would Have Amused You

I wanted to break into the morgue
with new pyjamas
champagne
a fat joint
white maltesers
intricate as we were
I wanted to hold your hand,
a blackbird
singing to you in the dead of night,
I wanted lorries
to line the streets
and honk their horns
by way of goodbye,
I wanted to say sorry
— instead,
I read poetry to a roomful of strangers
went home
to dark curves
in the road
to a fevery baby,
the next day
I went to your graveside
on no sleep
watched them lower you
from a distance
and at the wake
I was unwelcome
your mother insisting I was still the weirdo
that didn't dress like the other kids
but it was something more
something in me
she could see
but could never understand

(you did)
(we were)
and it never sat right,
in the graveyard
you sent
a breeze
to lift my hair.

We Are Haunted by the Dead

We are haunted by the dead,
his frozen uncle,
her slit throat in a phone-box
a knife she held
herself,
the one who held my hand
then jumped
at fifteen
on LSD — your body in the morgue,
I could not take pyjamas.
Outside on a street in the rain,
all the things unsaid
now unsayable,
cold sores on my lip
road snaking out around the city
like a noose
and for months I stood at 4 a.m.
looking out the window
the streets
always slick
with rain,
and dark and empty,
a curve at the end of my road
I stare at and know
impotence
to all but this ache.

I Can't Remember but the Body Can

My mouth is still hungry
for softness all these decades later

rain slides down the open window
like spermatoza toward

the curvature
of a bloody moon

while further up the building a man's voice
his low timbre, then he is laughing

steady as a morning,
where my son dreamt

of making a paper telephone
and I wanted to go out into the world

to tell everyone to quit the-fucking-shit.

Holy Joe

Homeless
on east & twenty,
sucked in
off the sidewalk.

Nostrils flared,
spicy calzone,
pizzeria
sweet goodness.

Holy Joe
on his altar
flipping dough.
sharing his warm heart

in witty banter
with homeless Aldo
— *gimme slice,*
Joe, me & Peter tight, man!

C'mon, Joe, you'll
never get to heaven
if you don't give me a slice
of pizza.

Faded nikes
dancing toward the door,
halting, backwards,
clumsy moves.

Holy Joe, smile
with your warm heart
& your pizza
safe in the oven.

Final word
tossed over his shoulder,
echoing through
the door.

Don't say I didn't
warn you, Joe,
when you meet Peter,
man, don't say!

I Love

Rouged-up
ladies
with handbag dogs
Noo Yawk
drawls
moth eaten furs
paper skin
and china bones
I want them
to take me home
feed me
apple pie
and gin
tell me stories
about the good old days,
at three in the afternoon,
show me their collection
of 1930s shoes
sit at their kitchen
table,
applying red lipstick,
still holding
themselves,
like
they did
50 years ago
on Broadway.

The Breakfast Room

A silver spoon
steals
the moon from morning,
haar-frost,
fields, sky,
concave halls
a woman
asking *what's on my eyelid?*
getting up,
sticking
her face right in
to where
I tried
a false
eyelash
on 'cos I used to think I'd be a swan
but fate
is kind of shitty.

I Sing You Old Blues Songs (Before You Get Here)

Kick,
kick,
kick.

You weren't interested
in what I was not,
or what
I had once thought,
(a crock of
crap for sure)
love was.

Pray,
pray,
pray.

You made me macrosmatic
(my second
heart)
blessed me
with bat-hearing,
hope,
and telepathy.

In the Middle of the Night I Eat Mirrors

The postman knows
I never sleep

jellied eels and champagne
I don't need

the soul ache
the fear

stubble
too rough for sunlight

hours of feed
the world asleep

stroke cheek to nose
and cry

I am a soul
gone to seed

the fictional stories
we tell ourselves

when we want out.

I See Her Every Day

Dear Woman in the Window —
you look like flowers.

You look like worry
replaced cigarettes.

Your baby sleeps easy
in between cries.

You watch the street, not drinking
or eating.

Your petals are thinner
than you ever thought could be true

of a living thing, and nobody
is a vase for long,

the smooth cracks
and the lake always waiting,

a reflection of wishes
as small as your dreams

have become, maybe to just go to a shop
on your own for five minutes

to walk the aisles
like a human yeti covered in hair

to hear the hum of fridges
rather than the crunch

of porcelain underfoot.
Dear woman in the window,

I see you every day
and I know you watch me

sitting out on the rooftop
at night while my child

dreams of grey men
who stand at our door

he says they whirl around
the world and they want to come in,

a boy whose hand I hold
two of us sat out on the back step

eating cheese sandwiches
or going to collect shells

the nicest
moments of my life,

I tuck him in each eve
like an owl high up in a tree

far from reptiles
or news bulletins

that seek to synaptically bruise
the error of psyche

I know you get this
I know you watch me.

Dear Woman in the Window
you must remember

how it is to be free,
even if only for the feel of it,

I sip a glass of wine
and we know each other is there

across the street, each
telling stories of star lore

to babes more precious
than time knows

you are still so carefully
separate, telling

the world it can knock
on your window

but it cannot make you
climb back down.

A Woman on the Telly Said,
If You Just Go Outside, Something Amazing
Always Happens

Dear Duck,
you are pretty slick
with your gliding
and your webbed
propellers
your verdant green
your peacock
shine
I have to say
you make me feel guilty
for eating your kind
and you can tell me if you like,
all ducks are not equal
nor even related
but haughtiness
won't keep your head
off the butcher's block,
and those
kids,
walking down the hill
for the duck race
have carnivorous teeth
and you are not a dinosauric duck
a giant with great serrated bills
you don't stride through posh streets
kicking down doors
demanding
tea
bandages and poetry,
the thing is,

duck,
you can glide away
but we are all much closer
than
we'd like
to perceive;
even you,
duck
are a bit of a Ruttle,
or a writer in a maroon suit
watching black & white films
through cheap
Japanese
binoculars.

Wonder Walnut

When you find your heart
is a walnut
withered and tough
when anechoic chambers
hold no malice
when the clatter is astounding
and vases impossible
and love
is wholly clueless.
The too great noise
is all vibrate,
and vibrato,
delta,
amphibic,
ungainly,
certifiable,
and you've even bought Wonder Woman
Converse certain of their cure
yet the feelings
only intensified
and you look down at her
smiling, right there on your feet
knowing she too felt unholy,
no lasso of truth
or indestructible bracelets
or projectile tiaras;
ever really fooled her
Aphrodite, Athena, Hercules and Hermes
had fuck all to do with her personal atoms
and of course there was the time
she had to scurrilously
revoke her powers
to stay in man's world
so she opened a Mod boutique

gave up mystic trinkets
for ninja chops
— the next time she was brought
back to life birthed
out of clay
her amazon women scattered
a trio of death goddesses
laced up their trainers
headed out in New York City
tae kill her once again,
resurrection is tedious
were the first words she said
when they brought her back,
this time a bona fide fucking goddess
daughter of Hippolyta & Zeus,
looking a bit too braw for someone
who's done bronze, silver and golden ages
who doesnae have for wonder girl
and has already brought up wonder tot
who nailed astral projection,
telepathy
mind control,
who knew God's blessing
was never upon her
and if it was she'd have wiped it off,
and when in the end they said she had to be
the most beautiful
woman in the world
and bring peace to our planet
she asked them to show her the contract
where she signed
for that on a dotted line
but they could never find it,
nor her tiaras
'cos she'd pawned them all
down Leith Walk
and they began to suspect

she'd never revoked her fucking powers
to stay
in
man's world at all.

What Happened?

What happened
to my unblessed womb?

What happened to agoraphobic
outings to Tesco

at midnight
wearing sunglasses and a hood

where I always saw the punk
with a suntan

and his goth girl,
what happened to the contract

I signed over to some guy
for ownership of my soul

because I was drunk
out my mind

and he said he wanted to own it
and I said — *fucking have it.*

What happened to silence?
What happened to Harper?

What happened to death?
What happened to thinking,

death was something
that would come much later?

What happened to bottletops
on trainers?

What happened to that girl
who built an entire attic wall

of Marlboro Lights boxes?
and I skinned up on her ironing

board, for an entire summer
until I could do it like sculpture

and each one had to be smoked
and it was what it was,

what happened
to shoulder blisters?

from the Scottish sun
in a caravan park.

What happened to jelly babies
(the kind you wore on your feet),

what happened
to becoming a swan?

What happened to the faraway tree?
What the fuck happened

to thinking I'd get there
and when I got there

I'd be alright somehow.

What happened to pink lightning
from Aimee's window

at night in the city
where the old Uncle

and the young General
would sell us knock-off tobacco?

What happened to tea-stained
mugs in other people's

flats that made me want to sneak
into their kitchen

and clean them, quietly.
What happened to all those never

consummated loves?
What happened to being unafraid,

what happened to VCRs,
speed-bombs,

swimming by eels in the river,

what happened to your voice?
Where did it go

when you left? You and me,
walking around a volcano

in a blizzard
holding our hands out

but we couldn't even
see them, both of us

sore with laughter
but never turning back

no fucking way.

What happened to dark
rooms and zombie games?

What happened to ten rounds
of tea and cigarettes?

What happened to dancing in
at the pirate graveyard,

to laying in the dark
looking into your eyes

to meeting each other in dreams
to only wanting you?

What happened to the feel
of your hands on my skin,

to that first
intake of breath,

your lips, parting my legs —
what happened to knowing?

What happened to conversation?
What happened to love?

What happened to the solstice?
What happened to covens?

That bump-nosed witch
who burnt himself out for good

doing astral projection?
What happened to New York,

that chicken at I.C. Guys
who poured us cocktails

at 6 a.m. watching *Nosferatu*,

who taught me to dance
on the podium, who kept

a bazooka in the garage,
who shot rockets with me

over the mausoleum
who scared the crackheads

and brought me flowers,
what happened to being a child

who could outsmoke mortal men?

What happened to hope?
What happened to cartoons?

What happened to teapots
being un-fucking-significant?

What happened to tortilla
chips being foreign?

What happened to time being linear?

What the fuck happened to my body,
my brain?

What happened to snow peaked mountains —
what happened to immortality?

What happened to bongs
in the back of camper vans,

What happened to Marshall stacks
on milk crates, the smell

of rehearsal rooms,

what happened to the tears
of poets, that slid

down their cheeks
as pure as gin.

What happened to

the first man
with a beard I ever loved

who I would have walked
the world twice over

for and still
came home to brew him tea?

What happened to
drowning in the bath

while someone kicked
in the door, and the night nurse

asking how many were left
now of my nine lives?

What happened to getting
a crowbar from a neighbour

at 5 a.m. to break into my flat
then just slipping my hand

through the letterbox
to open my door

for the next seven years.

What happened to that serial killer
skateboarder

in the piercing shop
where I doodled

in between customers
and chain-smoked

while selling dresses
I have to ask this, mon cherie,

what happened to you?
what happened to us?

What happened
to our tomorrow?

What happened, my love?

Her Favourite Suicide

Her favourite suicide
was leaping from the Forth Road Bridge
I didn't tell her
how I can't cross water
on foot
without serious unease.

She Thinks She's Doing It All for Love

She thinks a sideboard
can save
her from sadness,
she thinks her brittle
is balm
for gin,
she's contorting
trying to contain
the bile
the ill
enough hate to fill a handbag
pockmarks
for postcards,
if you ask
her, she'll say
she's doing it all for love.

Waverley Station

That pigeon over there

there

wi the
claw

and mangled stump
— rooty like a tiny tree,
aye, in it

— lives two crocodiles,
long as your thumb nail.

Of course they live in trees.
Crocodile trees.
Idiot!

See it, over there,
noh — there in the MacD wrapper,
oozy yellow pus eye,
red shot in the centre
half mohawk slicked up
he's coming closer,
fuck, aw fuck,
he's waggling
that stump
at you.

Fuck off ya skanky diseased rat wi wings, git away, ah mean it,
ah'll rip yer fuckin' heid off!

I know all about you.

Aye, ah fuckin' bet you do.

* *Italics, of course, represent pigeon speak.*

73

Hitching a Ride

When you don't even
have enough
energy
to write
when you feel so ill
you can't quite believe it
when you just want held
and someone
else
to make it okay
when you have decided
to view depression
as a spiritual journey
you are somehow
failing at,
because you had not realised
that you are
the spiritual journey
and depression
is just
hitching
a ride.

All I Want is the Meaning of Everything

I have been worrying
about the meaning
of the universe
pretty much
every day
forever
certainly
since I could pogo stick
most likely
before I could stand.

I used to stoat
around on stilts
in the caravan park
with the other kids
feeling I wasn't quite sure
I got
something
fundamental;
like what
we were doing on a planet
anyway.

Like how come
hearts beat,
and why the universe's expansion
has to reach a point
where it turns
back on itself
and how the meaning
of life
has fuck all to do with gobstoppers.

I might as well have worried about semolina
or a terrible slavery
kiss on a coal bunker
by a boy
with special needs
and sweat
and glasses.

A psychiatrist
informed me this existential
angst of mine
was common in depression
and I asked him
if that was perhaps a side-effect
of thinking,
of looking out the way
good and hard
to knowing your own mortality
is utterly
defined?

He wasn't sure
what to say to that.

I wondered
if they'd have tried to medicate
all the philosophers
Hegel,
Heidegger,
Herzog,
Dylan,
Gertrude Stein,
all the ones
who dared
to question
life.

The Second Person

When you have lost the book
you really wanted
to write in
(so you are scrawling in this one)
when you are questioning
the second person
and your Wonder Woman
Converse
have still to reveal
their powers.

They Say Witches Can't Cross Water

They say witches
can't cross water
and I know every time
I have to cross a bridge
I think
I can't do this,
panic
on first footfall
I don't look down
stay as far in from the side
as I can.

I've always had dreams
where I travelled
through time,
like the night I flew
across Southern England
at night
and a coven
caught up with me
in the air
shouting — *you can't fly solo*
it's not safe!
I told them I always flew that way
and to leave
me
the fuck alone.

And the coven master who said
I left enough energy
in stones
to start
fire,
all the time I drew a place

where I'd live,
a predictive child.

Or the dream where I went to a big house
with long steps
leading up to a row of french doors
and inside there were two old ladies
and upstairs four kids
were running around
and there was a gramophone playing in the corner.

The old ladies
were going to a ball
and I was there to babysit
and I said that I wasn't sure I could tell the children
about the spirits.

They turned off the record,
went over to a chest
and brought
out slate tablets
with ancient drawings.

The first was two girls dancing
they held up the second
asked if I recognised
that as well,
yes,
they said — *what is it?*

It's a famous nun,
who died
a long, long time ago.

They asked me
who this nun was exactly
I told them
it's me
— and they said,
see, you know exactly how to tell the children about the spirits,
and left.

Island

It makes you feel like you're on mild LSD,
& that isn't really
the way to describe it to the doctors
but when you take their tablets
light feels weird —
superimposed —
sort of patterned
a kind of imprint
and you are just unable
to imagine how to function
in the real world
through this superimposition
you google
your symptoms
and find millions of people
regularly feel like this
sometimes for years
and you imagine a small country
for all of us
where there are porches
and pretending you are okay
is illegal
and you find a soft blanket
and curl under it to sleep
and imagine yourself a cat
who has this unreal
feeling
that
will
not
go.

Sleight of Hand

You are in the garden
thanking god
for getting you through a day
where you felt
you might die
from the utter strangeness
but your son
wrestled you anyway
and the relief
to be near his solidity,
his irrepressible
ability to seize each day
just to hold him
just to say goodnight
sleep tight
sweet dreams
I love you
to kiss him
and tell yourself
that hell will never own you
if your heart
beats elsewhere
it can only play sleight of hand
and hope you don't look too clearly
— so, become a scientist
dear self
do what you gotta do
you have too much to give
and yes, it will be the hardest minutes
a woman has known
but there are others
who survive
every single-fucking-thing
and still get back up to live.

Fairy Muff

I move away
and go to art school
and loathe it
and I'm the oldest in my class
except for a woman
who changes
her name
and once
had an incident
with a famous
journalist
and her knickers
and bananas
and also some
guy who spent
eighty grand
on prostitutes and crack
which hasn't stopped
him hearing voices
and one day he reads out
the starkest
most majestic
gothic
poem
I have ever heard in my life,
and when a girl
in the class is
obsessed
by me being Scottish
and tells me how proud
she is to be from Norwich
and to be English

and do we live off their taxes
and do I get porridge imported
and what is haggis
and do they really deep-fry mars bars,
and I don't pay attention
too much
but every day
(for the first month)
at some point in class
I say — fair enough
so this girl
with her race pride
and her blonde ambitions
will shut the fuck up
but while I am saying
that, she actually thinks
I am
repeatedly
saying
— fairy muff,
and I think
how you would have liked that
and understood
why I stayed away
from the sane ones.

Adventurer of the Year

Sometimes I remember
a man in a kayak
with a smiley face
setting out to sail
he was going to be the first man
to sail 1600km solo
in a kayak
across the Tasman sea
and he rolled under waves
and storms
and swells
and he was only
56km short of Milford Sound
when they play his last message
and in his
voice
it's clear he has endured
(and seen) more than
most ever will
but he is going down
— so close to home,
almost reaching
where he set out in all true heart
to be,
so
courageous
to try for it with everything,
how utterly humane.

Submarine Circles

When you feel all things
at once
as an ache (a hardness, a knot) the creak

of bomb-torn seats
spires
of rubble

where remote controls
used
to sit,

when a mother
stands on a shore
holding her child's hand

making
jokes, kissing
his forehead,

trying so hard
to not let him feel afraid
as the boats sail in.

Sadness
is the only tune
the busker

plays on Porty
prom
while a submarine

circles
the bay
and all the fear

man has of the unknown
cannot be nuked
either way

what you tell
yourself is just
get through this minute

just be, and deal
with being,
make sure

those who love you
do not see
how deep the descent

or that each vault
has another
below,

because your arms
are still inexplicably
open and able

to hold,
you leave offerings
by the shore

in case a boat
arrives
before dawn,

or just so the sunrise
will see
someone knows

how beautiful it is.

Grains of Sand

When you walk along the beach
writing the greatest
poem
but grains
are drifting
south, they're billowing
behind you
like an Isadora
scarf
and the tide
knows how to pause,
it takes
and it gives
but it never remains.

You watch
a dog
walk through a puddle
reflected
long
spindly
salvador
legs.

The fine line
of futility
is absolutely
fucking
ceaseless
so you walk
until
your poem
is gone.

And you are
curiously

proud
to not sling the shot,
it has not been noted
or uttered;
its grains of sand
scattered
west, east.

You believe
in musical
prayers
so you play records
you play
songs
you listen with your whole life,
an old
soul
dimpled thighs,
you keep
your heart close.

Artists
are places
you go to;
galleries
are holy;
grace
is a bold heart,
a cracked
vase,
a missed
beat,
a fair sky.

The wine
will always be one more glass,
and Charlie
would get it

but he'd still
be a cartoon,
and when they put
you in a cell
you wrote in the dust
on
the floor
with your tongue.

When your body
always betrays you;
so you bring it stolen flowers
when you walk and you walk and you
walk
on
by.

When you've done what you had to do
to stay safe
from
doctors
when graveyards
are somewhere
you only go to dance.

When business
is so
big
it is putrefication,
when poets
are temples,
when
your pulse
falters,
when nobody hears you
because
it
is

the
dead
of
night.

When you
twitch
in the bathroom
for someone
for something
when the hot bath
sinks
and the dark
is
time.

When your
need
is immediacy
and tomorrow
is an afterthought
when
sandpipers
chatter
at midnight
on the shore
when time
is your companion
when you type
out of silence,
when
your
sun
is a pilgrim,
and knowing
is Norman,
when the heads of children
are

not
where
they
should
be,

When your sisters
are owned
and
others
make inroads
but you forgot
your bicycle,
when hell is something
everyone
should
believe
in.

When nobody
has a stun-gun
to falter
the armies,
when
the moon
is swollen,
and oranges
are just fruit
when your fridge
plays harmonies,
and walls can't contain you,

when Cupid
is a flasher
a taunter
a teaser
when he sits online
saying *onwards*

onwards
but you
travel
inwards
flying a feather;
when you text your friend
to tell him you
saw I Love You
chalked on
his doorstep
in a dream
and he says that it happened
that morning.

When
walking is lonely
but your beat
is
too
pure,
when the sea,
is parted
by
blood-tides,
and dawn
has
come
to
your
window
to show you
the
ceaseless;
when you wait in the pauses
for the next
crash
of
waves.

Glide to Hades

There are too many corpses
so burn me,
build
a pyre of books
and words from those who love me,
drawings
and secret messages,
finally,
place down
two shots of whisky
(good to arrive with something)
I won't wear
a wedding
dress,
don't ever
veil
me,
I'll take my chances,
neither lithe,
or unlined,
place candles on the water
glide me home
to Hades
before sunrise.

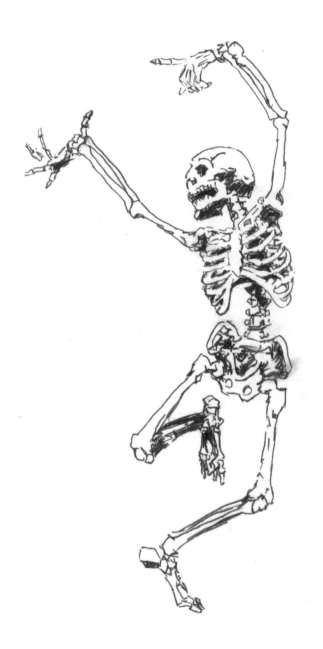

Collection II
The Dead Queen of Bohemia
(first published in 2010)

The Ether's Scribe

The ether's scribe
keeps her conch shell
ears
half tilted
always to the sea.

She sees phosphorescence
in tarmac
hears whale song in sirens,
motorway across the park
a waterfall's roar.

She sees hearts
pulse
through leathered skin
like it were gossamer.

She catches whispers
quiet as the fall
of ash,
or the entire world
reflected
in a single drop of rain.

The Bob Conn Experience

He'd been places, sex parlours and Woodstock and driving bareback
on a Harley across Canada in the 60s where the Indian girls would call

after him on the road, 'Why you call me honey in the bedroom and
squaw in the street?' and the men would fish barefoot off the rapids,

spears and salmon to glint in sun and his first armed robbery wasn't
really planned so, he found himself whistling, whistling in a cell

next to a native Indian wide as he was tall, eight years in Stoney
Mountain Penitentiary then kicked out of the country, sent on a plane

to a place where he couldn't get work or money and it was a matter
of months before he stole the shotguns (two from a farm) held up a

post office (got 25 grand) was grassed by his neighbour
and while digging up the guns saw a cop on the path and held the

long barrel up to the officer's head (another eight years) and then,
the day he got out of jail, they handed him jeans too big and trainers

with soles flapping away like loose tongues, they waggled all the way
to the halfway house, a basement dank as shit where he had to stay

for sixty days with three other prisoners just released, a paedophile,
a schizophrenic rapist, a murderer and Mr Conn, just your average

garden variety bank robber thief had seen worse and heard better
and the paedophile had questionable taste in shoes, ate everything

with ketchup: corn flakes and ketchup, burritos with ketchup, spam
and sweetcorn all covered in ketchup too and the schizophrenic

knew fifteen different ways to bring Satan through a crack in the wall,
like a great vagina of doom, portal of sorts, and while they sat and got

high and drunk, the murderer watched the lights of the buses streak by
the window like great electric eels in the night, their blue shimmering

the walls incandescent as his cigarette ash fell slowly to the floor.

For Wang Wei

Lanterns
brilliance
recedes,
clogs clatter
across ancient stones.

A little girl
hair shiny as oil
grips the brushwood door,
water-chestnut eyes
cast down.

The pickers pass
an' her lotus flower
so carefully
red,
blooms.

Wicker cranes
glide
out the mist
in hundreds
as white feathers
fall,
like obi
from the sky.

The First Time I Met My Dad

Yellow fingers
whisky dropped into a golden pint
I don't trust your hairline.

Shoes, leather
expensive but cracked
you light another smoke,

pull your jacket lapels up
tell me I look like a mother I've never met
but more beautiful.

10 Nicolson Street

Police keep knocking but they can't get in, this is junk territory,
stairwell like a no budget movie all needles an' spoons, a human

turd, plaster of porn, lights flicker on three times a minute, an' my
letterbox like a grim grin — swallows, announces with a thud the

arrival of the apocalypse, the debt collector's red alert, it does not
deliver words I pray for. I rip it open with a crowbar at 5 a.m.

got the shakes much? This is a tall box to live in so I dream up.
My fifth floor of madness, theatre bar across the street gawks over

wine and canapés for the famed Nicolson Street matinees: Junky &
the Jitter Bug, Schizophrenic & the Bondage Boy, Wife Beater &

the Bloody Sheets, fat corpse in my bath with a big fucking knife,
I've tried voodoo but the bitch won't go, I'm a girl that needs to hit

so I beat, beat, beat an old drum-kit set up where a sofa should be,
I play electric guitar in stilettos though no one can see me, I've a

smile like a bullet it's my secret stun gun, I walk the streets in
witches an' come back to where safe is four red walls and fifty silk

lilies stick out their tongues, bed is the only place, you can hang a girl
twice but only drown once, I close the door but they still send things,

a black rose, story sealed in wax, a silver dildo, a gun, a skeleton
hand, a Celtic ring, finest Bolivian, his wife's a witch — he says two

plus me makes three, freedom's got me absolutely fucking nowhere
but I don't have a price and I will never hear words I have waited forever,

hoping to be said and what I wanted was ecstasy but demons speak
through me, so I type, type, type for twenty hours a day, type as fire billows

across the ceiling, chars the walls black, turns all the mes of ever to ash.

The Devil Didn't Mark You,
Those Marks Came from the Man

You said guys liked it filthy, the filthier the better
you once got naked in a room of ten
to have a good time.

In the pub there were two and your legs parted
at 9 a.m. one fixed to your nipple
as you outstared the grey.

You had green eyes, teeth claws guts
you liked to fuck, you said
you couldn't get enough.

You had bloody crosses across your arms
and legs, said the devil marked
you as you slept.

We had peas for tea
washed our hair with stolen handwash
danced on ecstasy at the fair.

You were begging outside Scotmid,
on the nod, I couldn't stop,
I knew too well your pull to violence.

It's an I Thing

I is a terrible thing.

Always
leaving
or not leaving
long enough.

This I
I must
inhabit
will not rest.

It won't allow for the terrible baldness of eggs.

Old Man Whisker

Old man whisker
fastidiously inspects
each stranger
who sits
at the end of my bed,
he knows
apnoea asphyxiates
& the waken dead eat cornflakes
& neither of us mention the world outside
although we've both
heard talk,
for three,
eight,
twelve,
for sixteen years,
for twenty
— to him
a love sonnet,
a novel,
a play,
we have our eskimo rituals
and escape
is a suitcase
we unpack with words
until one day
a garden
& lavender windows
and just there on the doorstep
— an unmade crib.

The Byrons

Louche around Denmark Street guitar shops,
smoking roll-ups,
all smooth
dicks
&
narrow
hips
& drainpipes
& kohl
But where are their pistols?
Where are their gangrenous limbs?
Where are their monkeys, their mistresses,
their goats
and whores,
where are their Yen Tsiang,
broken
in
four?

Squirrels in the Walls

The mattress
in the neighbour's garden
is sodden
— mouldy
brown & gold leaves
blanket
the bits
where rain turned it black.

Squirrels
scratch in the walls
while we hibernate
in words,
our bedroom
cathedral
is
candlelight
safe.

The dealer
upstairs
vibrates
a low bass
and above that
a tap, tap, tap
as he cuts out deals
steady as a heartbeat
in the blood glow
of a womb.

The Snow Holt

The factories where coal
mines used to be, waft

winds candy sweet
across waste-ground,

clothes flap on makeshift
lines an' dogs bark,

Seven boys circle
me slowly

ma bare fists up,
incredible hulk

t-shirt kicked tae fuck
sodden wi slush.

An' they are tinkers
an' boys

but I am gypsy
just out the snow holt

like a white fox wi girl eyes
to glint as the winter sun fades

an' the factory siren blares
its bloody war cry.

Tree House

I
will
live
in
leaves,
with
just
a
typewriter
a
billy
can
sending
down
paper
aeroplanes
of
poems
and drawings,
smoking
while
stars
pick
their way
across
the sky
I'll
wait
up there
for
the
call of an owl.

Fat Isobel

Fat Isobel
waddles
along the hot tarmac
in her school girl
plimsolls
long
white
socks,
pleated mini-skirt,
unbuttoned-shirt
barely containing gargantuan
tits,
as all the metal blinds twitch
she tries to sashay,
irritated wives
turn up their TVs
while husbands pretend to look away,
and the laddies
don't give a fuck
that Isobel looks like a pale, untrimmed
lamb roast,
tied too tight,
they line up by her caravan
after ten when she's pished
in the scud
hairy fanny
oot, tits & tummy flopping
writhing on the grass
her man shooting
early DIY
pornos, all the boys by her fence

strain to get a better look,
wanking in a row
jerking like spastics
deep breathing creosote.

As the Gun Lock Clicks Off

I am still waiting
at sun up in doorways
in empty train stations
my footsteps
the all night echo
of a nobody,
age ten.

I am still waiting
in police cells,
strip
searched
while she is dead
in my doc boots,
my rage wasp fine
is burrowing.

I am still waiting
when the gang bang
goes disco,
on a bough of the elm
in some forest,
homeless and frozen
like an acorn
under October's moon.

I am still waiting
on the eighteenth
floor
Daddy,
locked in
for five fucking days
with evil, as the gun
lock clicks off.

5 a.m.

She is hoovering the road
at 5 a.m.
no cars
to get in her way
like errant slippered feet by the sofa,
she is naked
smoking
hoover in one hand
the plug trails along behind her
like an unwanted toddler
stupid and nappy wet
and hungry
and eager.
As the polis
pull up to the kerb
she is trying to polish the moon
just trying
to polish it pretty
as they cuff
her on the road.

Chimera

I'm only here 'cos you're the prettiest
girl I know, one green eye, one blue
you sell it for a line,
I have lines
but you won't buy them.

We blackout
like dominoes,
nobody knows what happens
in the dark
but I wake like I've been in a bath
candles biting
at the black
like vengeful halos.

Three guys lay like wax,
like we are a play they are dreaming,
we do not whisper
about the sinister
nature
of music,
about a ceaseless beat,
or how we don't exist
like people who've never been here.

Nine is the Number of the Universe

While you were the number nine,
I wanted.

I held that want in my hand
like a
glow
bug.

Like
the glow-bug
under the covers,
like
how I read
when I was little
and not allowed
to look
at the
 m
   o
     o
       n.

While you were wanted,
I was a red bug.

Blind with
nine
black eyes,
I read by glow-worm
tracing fingers
across runes,

I found
the faraway tree,
pulled up
its
l
  a
   d
    d
     e
      r
       s
stuck my fingers
up at you.

The Second Time

We were crossing bridges.
your side of the river,
my side of the river
on a boat
Gin & London's finest,
back over again.

I saw your smile
through the crowd
before you got to me,
a flash, a reflex
I wore the stockings
just for you,
on the bus
the looks
in the street
but yours was the one
I was seeking.

There was a band
on the bridge
trumpet going,
our first words
were notes.

Your shoes
clicked
and later
in the hotel room
I listened to the street
waiting to hear that click,
reprints staring
at me laying on the bed.

Absinthe Abattoir

Fishnets
fifties
knickers
boys in black nail varnish
axe wielding sociopaths
who couldn't stand people
but made them dance anyway
we
p
  l
    a
      y
       e
        d
like we meant it
our clothes stank of rehearsal
rooms,
concrete bunkers
dust
on valve amps
sweat
and cigarettes
we tied
each other up,
or walked
cobbled
streets with guitars on our backs
k
  i
    s
      s
       e
        d

only strangers
in
the absinthe abattoir
where
they
pound
down
the
bones.

The Bee Hummingbird

There's a spectre
in the attic
tap tap tap tapping
bending me a Scold's Bridle
out of metal bars,
complete
with metal asse's ears,
he welds it with rust
from the water tank
slips the harness
across my sleeping head
slips a metal rod
in my mouth
clamps it wide,
so my voice
can't get out.
He greases the lock
with butter,
smiles
swallows
but his mask can't contain
a two inch hummingbird,
who flies from my larynx
at dawn, sings
to the sun
of her sorrow.

The Happening

This life
happened at me
like a runaway roller-coaster
on crystal meth,
like the buffalo's
thundering
off Head Smash Rock
so the Indians could skin 'em
by the hundreds,
drag 'em home.

It happened like a fucking meteor
in my crater brain
so I happened right back at it,
I happened it by the hair,
I happened holes
in its murderous heart.

I happened it upside down
and sideways,
I shot a bazooka
up its hairy arse,
wrestled it naked in the mud-pit
dropped water words
on its head
in
an incessant
mercenary
drip.

This life which happened at me,
I happened right back at it,
I happened it under
the fucking table
and then some
and how.

Fiddler's Green

I sit under a black sun for seven hundred days,
drink the blood from my veins
the damp from the walls
I cradle six aqua eggs,
empty as the sea.

Chimney rattles like umbilical tin,
I make it into a bazooka
march barefoot
out onto a bald lawn
and aim it at the moon.

Drainpipe slides down the wall
like a dancer parting her legs
to dark city beats
sirens wail like banshees,
the stutter of a gun.

I am irredeemably orphan,
three-parts witch
the moon a silent O
as I salute the endless,
sip homemade juniper gin.

I build a fire from forty suitcases,
light it with a ticket
to Fiddler's Green,
the devil walks by
an' tips his hat
'cos he knows what I've seen.

The Dead Queen of Bohemia

She cut the engine
stole into Mexico

wearing yesterday like a veil
wearing a black mask

fire for hair
the silver flash

of scales on rattlesnakes
shaking out there in the desert

shaking with rage.

Collection III
Urchin Belle
(first published in 2009)

Glencoe Mizzle

You are a Celtic Tánaiste,
the first crunch of frost
a whorl of midwinter mist
silently silvering the moss.

You are bracken crackling,
a peaty alchemical gold
a thread of smoke spiralling
a thistle on a pebble shore.

You are a nest in the Oak
a twig that holds up the moon
a tail-flick of saltwater smolt
silhouette of a castle's ruin.

You are Glencoe mizzle soft,
a curlew's cry across the loch.

Brooks & the Bishop Moon

Our wood hearts clunk-thud,
our steel curls scour stone

our glass tears glued on,
our cloth tongues fuzz wool

our black eyes pour oil,
our cut stings, lick clean

our blood lies so vein thin,
our moon is not a full stop.

In an Old Basque & New Knickers
on the Thrown-Away Theatre Chair

I sit in the hallway
quiet, on a Victorian
chair, red satin swirls
under pale bare.

The second cigar
an' the wait,
my legs apart
enough,
my knickers
clean, enough.

Rivulets trickle
unseen in the shower
Cuban smoke unfurls,
scents the air.

My hair black,
my heartbeat slow
soft skin, one nail
chipped red, tapping.

My want torturous.

My wait willing
the city hum
somewhere
out there.

An' your key
loud in the door
your tread
on the stair.

Your voice low,
telling me to part
my legs wider,
to pull my knickers
to the side.

In Woods You Wait

Would that I would,
— would that I would,
so fucking badly.

You send me a purple sky
wild deer
stars an' a moon.

Silver dust spirals
through woods, you inhale
the dust, send it to me.

You wait in the woulds.
In woods you wait
on bracken

swollen
by river, by rain
it seeps through your thin

but your bones don't care.

Would that I would
an' you know it
you wait.

You carve
let me
in the forest

a wooden heart
— gouge
across knotted scars.

Would that I would,
— would that I would
so fucking badly.

The King's Chamber

Enter the pyramid, out the haze
bent double in corridors dim,

this was not built for humans,
we are not wanted here; press on.

Vertical slope of the great gallery
musty stale, worn wooden holds

in stone silent with the secrets
of centuries. Climb to the chamber

doorway, I turn like a key that fits,
skirts swishing to the sarcophagus.

Air vents filter the lilt of ancient
Egypt outside, cows an' slaves

at market, bells clink round bare
ankles. Crowd's reverent murmur

rises as camels trail out the desert
mouths chewing, red tassels sway.

Twelve armed warriors flank
the King, I stand in his chamber

with my home cut hair an' burnt
feet, eyes closed, jus' listening.

After the Sword Years, Mid Pink Gin

You met me in my time of want
but my shades were drawn

an' the words were all.
I had fought and slayed

the dragon,
drank his blood

pounded his bones to dust,
fine silken grains that slipped

through my fingers again and again.
I wore his scales as armour,

impenetrable as a heart.
I told no one yet the first time we met,

you said 'Your lips are stained
the sweetest red.'

Your fingers in the black of my hair,
plucked a glittering scale,

I flicked my tail,
then fled.

On a bridge of light
I stopped the view

where we would have kissed
had I been free,

my scales fell one by one
to the river,

turn to silver fish.
Now you send words

to steal my want.
My un-armoured

heart hammers,
I throw up shutters

on windows an' doors
yet the nails of steel

melt like the kiss
your eyes

promised me.

Empty September Caravan Rentals

I was twelve,
and he was going to die a horrible death.

Lipstick houses
an' a peace symbol

an' a hangman,
pictograph

the empty
caravan rental wall,

sealed with my signature kiss.

I lie on the floor
in the dark,

breath held
while the dog

an' the security man
blink torchlight.

Local rag on the floor
warns of paedos,

my face
stares out

for seven days,
I am still missing.

The curtains smell
an' the carpet smells

an' my desperation is quietude.

I exist on fizzy juice, fags, crisps
an' the rustle of trees.

I wear the river I bathe in.
The metal door clicks open.

He, has brought an audience.

And I am twelve, and he has not yet died
— a horrible death.

The Sick Kids

Have parents who visit
an' try an' get *little* Edward,
little Clare an' cunt Catherine
to not look
at the twelve year old
'Cos they know why she's in.

White curtains
box my dreams
'till the fifth day when I wake,
tubes *sprouting* out nostrils,
needles for veins.

In two days I can stand, drag a bleep, bleep
around it *cleans* the *poison out.*

Sit on a tiny chair in the play area
knees like a giant
my exhale
sounds like *suici,*
suici, sueecii, sssuuicide,
I make the parents of real children edgy,
this bed is a metal jail.

Listen to hospital radio it's DUMB AS FUCK
watch the kids whose *families*
come an' go,
speak
to the social worker

an' the fat paedo shrink
who stinks of chocolate and shit.

Pad outside, barefoot, not a teen yet,
'*D'ya like* ma paper ballgown?'
The orderlies like it, they like it a lot,
I smoke whatever they give me
blissful dizzy,
by the door
a blue blue sky
an' wispy trails of clouds.

Watch — They Get High off This

Your girl fists pound
hard as a man's punch
'Fae the home?' they say,
you smash in, split bone.

They stand, smoke, take bets,
ten or five
the girl you haul back off the road sobs
an' begs, feet push on ground.

RIP ear, blood, you punch in again,
she's OUT
the dark CAN'T stop,
TOO FAR GONE they say
eyes slide to me an' I stare back.

Watch — they get high off this,
they LAUGH like TIN then stop.

'If you don't STEP IN she'll die'
they try to plead nice
but with glints in their eyes,
rain spits, lamps curve to see.

Her head limp, teeth CRACK,
scud off stone phlegm flies,
I step in from the back
take your arms, talk fast an' low
arms of four, now two, pound an' slow.
Watch — they get high off this,
blue lights in the dark
flash flash flash
an' the wails
wail, I take your hand.

Watch — they smoke us into woods
wheels screech, hands point
but we are gone.

You shake by my side,
match flares
you suck in smoke
I stroke your skin,
leaves soothe an' whish by,
jail will not TAKE you from me.

You Broke Every Knuckle
on Lamp-posts on the Hill

Spirals of light
busy the air
before dawn,
tracers of colour,
you clenching your fists.

Each knuckle
raw
meat
purples
an' half dried blood.

My bare feet twitch
under un-smashed
windows.

I am
not thinking
of school or care.

Beyond the veil
is my domain,
and
you dare
to meet me here?

Where's your sawn –
off shotgun now, my love?

You send me the thought
cool an' clear
as the river,
hold it out
to me like flowers.

If I can't have you
no one will.

142

The Empty Vase

The eighth floor of the tenement view
sliced in three, an' in the centre you sit
naked on a table, legs in lotus, drinking light.

Petal hair an' opal eyes, your fingers
see through, you lick their salt, saliva
scents dry air, the vase contracts, a sigh.

Black clouds settle low around the volcano
outside, crags with their jagged ancients
grumble, a flash of blue, further even than waves.

You, naked silk, drinking light orange to grey,
you're bone-thin, pretty evermore, purple petals
for hair, the empty vase, iridescent perfection.

You incite storms to gather, veins see through
as octopi, petals falling slow into the vase,
browning as the view beckons in the night.

We must follow our stupid hearts, so you sleep
quiet as night an' just as true, nestled in petals,
glass folds around your dreams, tucks you in.

Gringo's Whiskers

He burns them on a candle
lies on his back
an' snores
later he'll wake
an' we'll kiss like eskimos
he'll watch tennis
I'll make us chicken for tea
an' tell him again
he is the best
of all the Gringos
an' how grateful I am he never left
not when the moon
hammered on the window
for bone
or when the roof
double dared me
and the cartoon
became Monday
not when ghosts
came to stay
an' refused the living
at the door
not when sea
threw me to sky
or when the fridge
only held a microphone
not when I got back
from New York
and set the sky alight
held a three year chat with death
slept only
with spirits
an' sold rings of tin
for gold.

In My Dream

The gypsy girl
thunders by on a runaway rocking horse,

her mustachio'd cigarettes twitch,
quit nicotine, refuse matches.

In Montreal the whisper
Ménage à trois, s'il vous plaît?

I hear this as they lay her casket
in frozen ground, branches stripped bare

no leaves or mulch to feed the soil,
grey sky ignores my anthracite eyes,

torn tresses by the gravestone
flutter in the breeze.

Councillor

He has a small apologetic cock
epileptic
spasmodic
crying its glue,
she doesn't care
she hates fucking anyway.

He jabs it in her throat
shoves an' grunts an' sniffs,
turns her over, thumbs
grip in anger
purple blooms mottle
over yellow blues.

The snap of rubber,
cars beep beep
headlights slink
along the walls,
white hungry eyes,
looking.

Fists clench.

Pound pound pound,
tick one minute
tick two,
muscles shudder
release,
condom slumps
to the side.
His trousers hunch

on the chair,
his shirt
spreads its arms wide
his pointy shoes
say *we are leather,*
we do the Times
cryptic crossword.

She doesn't care
if he does Tim, Tom and Tit
and most likely he does,
but this is her hour
and she'll take every last note he has.

The Other Night; Once Again

My teeth fell out.

My heart ran,
screaming
for the hills.

A notion
wisped by.

I grabbed on,
wrung it into
a skyscraper.

Threw myself
from the battlements
only to find
that I
can
fly.

Lituya Bay

The unseen swell
of ocean black.

Blood soaked into sand
as a three year old
drops his bucket
runs up a still
silent beach.

A whisper on the leaves,
glint of sun on steel.

Birds surf waves
of wind
in silence.

Wood creaks
on a porch
fifteen miles
inland of the bay,
the blind man
rolls his cigarette,
arm hair raised.

Babylon

Blinking
gummy
wrinkled
STARING.

They share a glance
& turn back
to watch.

Would feel no surprise
if one drew out
a bag of popcorn
to chew on.

Their bar stools
creak in approval,
Ya don't
get fresh tuna
round these parts much, you see.

They exude a potent
aroma of tired flesh
an' weary bones
seeking
some escape
from the sentence
time has instilled.

Shiver.
Order a drink.

Light a cigarette,
steadily aware
of their longing gaze,
yearning to touch
smooth skin
& not yet
fully broken
dreams.

Sedna Be Free

Haze
hovering
over everything.

The scientists
found a planet
an' called her Sedna.

Who would be a planet
named by scientists?

Pretty boy
on the radio
telling me he loves
the tiredness of my eyes,
the motion
of my pen.

Men in the street
drilling their cocks
into the tarmac.

Who would be a pavement
with nowhere to go?

The lady with the cards
who cannot
take whisky
any more informs me . . .

'The red fox
is the one
to whom
your soul
belongs.'

I tell her,
'He is with another.'
I tell my friend,
'He's with another.'

Haze settles on the steeple
as the woodlouse cries.

It Should Be Dark, So You Can See

There is always a scene
you didn't see last time.

A horse wearing a dress,
a fold in the curtain
that wasn't there,
an' a line
you never heard,
delivered as she adjusts
a stocking you swear
she didn't wear
before breakfast.

The grey skies of the first time
blink to orange glass.

That celluloid breathes,
recoats the dream
in a silent whirr
while you sleep.

The barley fields
sway in waves,
an' his submarine
is a burnt out car,
the bombs he lobs
are apples whose stalks,
he pulls out with his teeth.
Bee lady of murk marches
with her square face,
an' her widow scarf
an' that one
creamy red engorged
eye un-blinks; your fear perceptible.

The room should
be dark, so you can see.

So you can hear the score,
as shadows leap
an' pirouette
along the walls,
an' kiss through all the adverts.

And you too,
are in the silent
shadow film,
wigged in smoke curls,
lifting a cup of tea that points in disbelief
as horns grow out your ears
an' your nose falls off.

You are different,
each time you watch.

Same jeans but sore heart,
chipped nails, patting the cat
glasses on, after she died
eating popcorn, snow
an' rain an' hail outside
an' that scene you didn't notice
the last seventeen times,
materialises

An' the same scenes,
they too are different.

Put a Record On

I was high for the first time.

Half a bottle of paracetamol,
heart tablets, something for angina
or rickets or neutering rats.

Malibu out the sideboard,
still sticky from New Year.

I won't ever be thirteen,
I will always be a virgin.

I slip a record on,
music to die to.

The turntable spins,
disco lights
on my speakers
flashing
red
an' then yellow
an' green an' then blue.

Even the Last One Left When I Called Time

Every house I ever lived in,
families paid to keep me,
lovers glad to leave me,
adopted folks who
never knew me,
men who tried
to marry me
women
an' friends who
left my bed.

Not one of those
claimed me
truly
as their own,
not so this scared
stupid
little heart
would always know.

An' you say
the right lines
you meet my eyes
an' don't walk away each time
I plead fear.

No one ever said,
'Stay.
Don't go.
I won't let you,'
or if they
did, they
said it
real

quiet,
hoped I
might agree.

I am not an agreeable girl
in affairs of the heart.

I need a love that's real enough
to scare me,
true enough
to maim me
for the scars it needs to slip by
run too deep.

No Stars Pension in Downtown Cairo

The cat yowls at us,
hackles
like a matted
fur collar coat.

It will die in this heat.

Room 453 is ours,
an off green,
shower cubicle in the corner
curtained by lace
that once was white.

Someone has drawn
a heart, in the dirt on the wall.

Tinfoil holds the air conditioner
together, I lay on the bed
think of heroin
an' cerise,
an angel with dirty feet
in the photograph you take.

Keys in art deco wardrobes
wear dust
an inch thick.

Higher still a gap
gapes into a grin as I sleep.

Down scurry scarab beetles
blues an' greens,
through bare
floorboards,
out cracks in the walls.

Cairo has seen this before.

They are here for you and I,
come to pick our bones
clean
of a love
we will soon,
no longer know.

Abstruse

The guns are too shiny,
we'll melt 'em in the microwave.

I'm on the loo, skinning up,
coming down.

You in the bath blowing
smoke-rings, underwater

'D'ye hink they took
ma looks?' you echo.

I lick the fag, rip an'
lie, to your dropped smile.

You got off the game today,
sweet sixteen, a neophyte.

My purple eyes swollen
shut, blissfully blind.

Locks of hair fall on lino
your head newly shaven,

Empress of future castle king,
pierce my skin again with your instinct.

Late Night Visits

Take it to the altar
an' lay it down

sipping homemade
cherry wine

as your friend's
prick says,

— *don't upset the witch*
she's having

an off day

inevitable then
screaming

takes only
five minutes

to ensue
she informs

she has a gun
claims my anger

makes me sick
her black cat

closes wearied eyes
the room stops

silent, poised
tense

on the brink
of no return.

Shit Ma Ru

Murker Lurky's
at the bus stop
wearing nuhin'
but Voodoo Dolly-Anna's
scanties, he's singin'
la la la la la la la la
throwin' all the moves
like a bitch
on ketamine.

Wendy tongues the light lush
like a hot rod baby, all the boys sigh.

To the spaceship, James,
I'm late for jail,
or jus' court, let's be hopeful.

What's that you say?
Fourteen's an earner?

True, but not for you, I'd be my own boss,
whips
an' chains
an' things, what you smiling at? Prick.

Gotta float,
whip you later
my poor pathetic Bolivian king.

The Pig and the Polis Lights

The pig strip-searches me behind
Scotmid, two old ladies walk by, stare
at my stiff nips, pretend not to see.

Pig hisses *bout my kind* marches
me to the station, slams me in a cell.
I stand there silent in mismatched

bra an' pants as she walks round
an' round an' round, ma skin white
blue, like the spill of the moon

on ma knife as I crouch on her
pig car a half hour before sunrise.
While the houses sleep I hum,

'hink if I were owned she wouldnae
search me but there's perks to bein
free, I unscrew my third polis

light, run barefoot into woods
Lothian Borders Police stickers
trailing behind. She's at the home

before school oinking like a freak
staff search ma room, find nothing.
I do the next at dawn to birdsong.

The fourth on Sunday as the church
bells ring, the Vicar's son's ma dealer
he's hid everything, reckons ah'm

ah hero an' should smoke for free.
The next day the camera appears,
a sci-fi eye by the station door

but I am not afraid. I do a hooded
attack at half five, takes forty minutes
'cos they used screws an' araldite.

They lift me at the pavilion, stoned
immaculate, they say the Eye
has a zoom an' I'm going to secure.

Can you bring back any stolen items,
Miss Fagan? I ask for ten minutes
they gimme two, my dealer sniggers

by his door, loads them in ma arms,
the giggles get me at the station,
the pigs are waitin', drinkin' victory

tea. I step up to the counter, neatly
line up six neon pink glittery lights
they all fall silent, I look up an' smile.

Epilogue

Journey to the Centre of the Earth

The sound of a bird,
sore head

remembered how it was to be,
to think my older self would save me —

What purple!

I didn't like to paint any more.
If I liked. I liked. If paint, I would — I didn't.

I dreamt of you
but you were lemon in the brain

I gave you a loudspeaker and asked you to whisper.

You came to inspect me
in my most vulnerable state

I wouldn't have been surprised at all if you'd staked me.
In that space where a room was,

where I met the man
and the maker and the small dot.

In that room. Which every room thereafter was only a replication.
In a room

where I sought myself as a thing
that would still breathe

— breathe still.

You were colder than a lover.
In every room I was a dot.

I sought to draw oxygen from the atmosphere
— inflate the lungs before dawn.

In every room there was another room, smaller without windows
and after a while no doors either.

In that room where I was dark
and all of time

formless
without teeth or lips or hair or hands.

Dot, dot, dot.

Somebody told me the heartbeat I heard was mine
and if I didn't claim it they'd put it in the trash

I heard trash belonged to another country but I held no alliance
no class — this wasn't school

I wasn't a lesson
if that heart was mine I should put it in a jelly bean bag

walk it to the shops, walk it to the park
lay it by swings so it could beat in peace

so it could beat, so it could be seen
so I could see it beating and know in fact

what it is to be.

A dog would walk by and sniff it,
wouldn't he and I'd tell him,

don't go in that bag there is a heart in there
and of course there would be a heart in the dog as well

and it would beat and beat and beat
as if beating was just the thing to do,

and later there would be issues with breathing,
with taking breath in, with letting it back out.

It would happen on a bridge until I'd know
that going out among breathing people

wasn't something I could do any more.

I would have to stay in a room. A red room.
A room with fifty white lilies

sticking out their tongues,
a room that sounded like a phone box

a room that had a dead lady sitting with a big knife
and my wet towel on.

Give me back my wet towel — I would have said that to her
had she not been dead and more importantly

tooled up with random sizeable weaponry.
Instead I lay in my bed in the dark of night

with a pen in my fist.

I would tell her, *the pen is a weapon*
I would tell my cats, *look at mummy using this weapon*

They would listen to my scratch-scratch
of pen or pencil or tip-tap tip-tap

I was jazzed, goosed, hooked,
I was high on the contact, me and words

they weren't scared and I was umber.
I was ready to give everything to something

and the words picked me out a hat
I was a conduit in the room

a conduit in the city

where ambulances had whale sounds
held inside their armoury,

where whale sounds were all around
and people were drinking

where bars were musicians
and poets were wankers

where some pavements were walked on
and others were not

where a hotel had a roof and a sniper
and a princess

and all the things that should be real — were real.
They were the bird man and his jackets

and how it is to sleep in doorways
near anywhere that a fan might blow hot air

I knew the hotels that did that
I knew how to hide from waiters

having a sandwich with the bird man
and being chastised in a classroom

later by someone who didn't know
I knew what it was to live without walls

and I felt sorry for him,
he who didn't know that doors and walls crumble

and everything is temporary!

Who didn't know a 19 year old
can be an angel but if their sight is too pure

they won't know how to breathe
because their entire being kens

toward seeing,
and all around

a globe appeared to be turning
I travelled down to the core of the Earth in the off days

in my off way, casually, sideways as a crab
in case the layers of earth

cottoned on to what I was doing.

I donned glasses, plastic, perspex, visors, balaclavas,
I took the balaclavas off

I wasn't going down there to rob the joint,
I wasn't going down there for time travel

I wasn't hoping for tea and scones at the centre of all being
I was just irritated by the inability

the surface layers
the onion of being

and all those people who never peel that first oily, crackly skin
I, of course, a shedder of layers

shedding, shedding, shedding!

So, I could tunnel down
through the core of my building

like a concrete apple
that housed far too many junkies

and when I got to the basement
and all those needles

I turned them on their end
so they could tunnel too

up above people were walking, walking,
stopping, looking, meeting, phoning,

drinking, eating, shitting, laughing,

hoping, crying, working, working, working,
when they were working and when they were not working,

most especially when they were yesterday
and all those footsteps grew faint

while I was underneath tunnelling,
tunnelling, tunnelling, tunnelling,

a child from a coal mine,
a demon with a mission,

a postal letter in human form
and heading straight for the core

with the pen.

Knowing earth and soil
noise, the bang, the scatter — wordless formation

174

knowing — nothing existed long before I did
always holding a little

of that nothing inside
until it becomes too much

and I have to get on a bicycle
but right now heading for the core

one sight
straight down,

blinkers on nothing else will do!

You can't go halfway,
don't lie to yourself for god's sake

you have to keep your own secrets
you must have your own back

if you don't then your shadow
will claim them as her own

and you know what a fabulist she is
you know how she is

with her tickety-boo
and someone rightfully asks

what kind of fuckery is this?

But you and you and you
are in all truth

better with your tentative breathing,
your tunnelling, tunnelling

undistracted by layers of volcanic
yellow that glow, glow, glow

in the dim
unconcerned by hands that pat

you as you tunnel by
little hands, big hands, eyes hoping you'll look back

but modern people don't look
come on, we know better

than that, and we are all professionally raised by the state
— that's something, isn't it?

A handstand in formation
be upright or be afraid

and you are just an ambassador
of connection in a time

of great separation so don't be stopping
especially don't be stopping

all that tunnelling with a pen
is making your shoulder ache,

that injury from forever, that injury so knotted,
into limbic locks so acute

it shortened your bones!

So you would walk
as if one leg was shorter than the other

as *if* one leg was
— it was of course, you'd never lied about it

dip at the top of your spine
like a slide for a ping pong ball

and almost there at the centre of the Earth now
where men thought they couldn't go

with their silliness and violence
their unthinking

with the small clam and the anvil.

And you of course can remove the moon from the sky
you have done so many times

she is happy in your pocket
radiant in your mouth, you let her float out

and it's not like she doesn't go there willingly
the moon is a sucker for poets

and when you cross over,
it won't be family it will be Gertrude and possibly Arthur

or Kurt, or Cassandra, Gringo, Chiquita
if you are lucky — the best friends you lost

and right there at that moment
you have no choice but in stopping.

The rock, the rock, the stone, the final layers
chip, chip, chipping away

a road of chippings behind you and your pen, look at it!
It wasn't meant to be a digger

except of course it was, it is,
that little nib, still look at you now

right down there where the wild things won't go
the core, of the core, of the core, of the core,

where basking sharks tell tales of what?
The beginning of time?

You'd suggest we all just start over but who are you to be rude.

There doesn't appear to have been a person
in human form here before

the centre of the Earth
is listening

and what do you have to offer?
A breath so light it won't flutter the still.

Right down here
in the root of our planet

the hard bang, carbon and matter
there is no such thing as being — thing like

don't imagine there is anything galactic about it!

When you rub dirt from your eyes
you are not surprised to find

the centre of the Earth
is a walnut

withered and tough
and pulsing

anechoic and beating
of course, that beat, first beat, last beat,

in between all is beat
and all there ever was, was beat,

you first heard it in the dark!

You wonder how it is you came to be here
on a Sunday morning,

should have just stayed home and remembered
now to tunnel all the way back

without turning around.
this tunnel is not wide enough for turning

so it is feet first,
toes like fingers

climbing, climbing
tunnelling back —

toward the light!

Acknowledgements

I'd like to thank, note or otherwise raise a glass to anyone who let me read poetry to them at four in the morning.

Also, all the people who encouraged my poetry including: Blackheath Books, who first published *Urchin Belle* and *The Dead Queen of Bohemia*; Geraint Hughes, who accepted my first submission as a scrunched piece of paper shoved at him in passing after a reading at the Betsy Trotwood many years ago.

Tangerine Press, the *Scotsman*, *3AM Magazine*, *Gutter*, *Dogmatika* and any of the other litzines or online sites who first published some of these poems, thank you.

Cherry Smyth — you always inspired me. Tracy Bohan, thank you always. Nathan Thomas Jones, I raise a hat. Mrs Kite, Shirley Allison, Kevin Williamson, The Coach & Horses in Soho, Degenerate Sweethearts & Rebel Scum, Joseph Ridgwell, Alan Warner, Neu! Reekie!, Ali Smith, Helen Oyeyemi, Niall Griffiths, Russ Litten, Adelle Stripe, Edward Crossan, Gerry Cambridge, Word Power Books, Jen Hadfield, Christian Downes, Aimee Jack, Michael Pedersen, the Hopes, the Kellys, Susan Kane, Bob Conn, Jason Arthur, Tom Leonard, Bob Dylan and all the other many dead and living poets, musicians, artists, writers, friends, radges, strangers, pets, countries, hairdos, drumkits to whom I owe gratitude for sharing their talent, friendship and wine.

These collections are for all the urchin belles of forever and both the un-dead queens of bohemia as well as those on the other side, a wee (big) salute from me to you.

Soho, you were beautiful, Cairo, NY, Berlin, Cape Verde, Paris, Toronto, Athens, Montreal, Italy, Frankfurt, Sibenik, Edinburgh, the Highlands and all that falls between, and especially thank you to any library van that ever let me borrow a book, and of course the ether, who gave me this here life.

Most importantly I would like to thank everyone at Polygon, especially Edward Crossan, all of the team who worked hard to put together a beautiful book and who understood this from the start. Gerry Cambridge, who patiently went through this collection and Edward who did the same, several times.

Nathan, who used to carry my first book around on the tube like an iPod and whose drawings now adorn these pages, thanks for all the amazing art, I'll meet you in the ballroom, waltz-step, one-two, quick-step, to the side!

To anyone who ever stood in a dark room and listened to me read, or picked up a book — thank you.

I was asked several times, why publish these now? I suppose there are various reasons, but one is that I have taken charge of my space, time, location (as Burroughs suggested) and I am ready to stand by this work. Also, for me this is a line under the last few eras. It is time to start over. I have been writing poetry for thirty years and these are just some of the ones that have survived. These made it to the final cut but the majority did not. Someone suggested to me that you are meant to wait until you are sixty to put out a collected; I suppose it depends how many lifetimes you have already accrued and whether you believe you'll make it to the end of the rainbow or not. I don't believe in rainbows. I believe in the dog I can hear barking outside. I believe in the grey clouds on the horizon. I believe in you. I believe in me. It has taken me a long time to be able to say that with conviction. My poetry has developed to a specific place in my life and the next body of work will be different. These poems deserve to stand alone in a space that is whole and of itself. I could not have written many of them now, I have been sketching out my life in words for ever, but as I change, the way I write does too and I am more than happy to stand up for any of those that are a little rougher or meaner, or even more hopeful around the edges. This is a progression of a voice. These are depictions of moments in time. I have travelled my whole life. There has been one constant in words. Poetry picked me.

I used to submit to some poetry publishing houses and often got the impression from slightly more 'conventional' or 'contemporary' poetry editors, i.e. the supposed keepers of the realm, that what I write is not poetry at all. I suggest, to those chosen few, that they reascertain ideas of ownership and truth right across the board. If you only keep adding milk, brothers, it surely makes for pallid tea.

Thankfully I found many people to work with who just get it; if you are a poet who is unsure if there is any place for you at all, I suggest you seek out the same.

In conclusion, I started writing poems when I was seven years old for no particular reason and I never stopped. I could say that there was no reason, but perhaps it is more accurate to say for someone who was voiceless in many ways — putting that first word down on a page and seeing it as a real thing compelled me. However, it didn't make me a poet. That is a different thing altogether. I was always like this. Drawn to words and cadence and discord. I had a ceaseless need to take snapshots of life in words. I listened to everything. The wind on the leaves. My heartbeat. Others' sadness. The too great silence. I couldn't help it. That is what defines a poet's calling. I was always a little brittle around the smooth and sublime, my eyes propped open by little marching matchstick girls, unable to get through a day without writing.

This poetry owes a debt to all the books that allowed me to escape and be and feel, the ones that taught and sustained me, creeped me out, made me laugh, kept me, were there when I needed them and had no hesitation in challenging me. I owe you big time. I always thought I was a writer (even if nobody else knew I wrote) right from the start. After the first little book of poetry I wrote when I was seven (dreadfully twee it was I must say) I wrote daily for thirty years. I have filled books and books and books of poems, drawings, essays, diaries, stories, plays, sketches, manifestos. I burned twenty of those books a few years ago. It takes a lot of petrol to burn that many A4 journals. These are a few of the poems that survived a lifetime of transience. I considered writing a proper introduction to frame these collections but decided, as with everything, it is better to let the work stand alone. If anything, they are a manifesto of otherness looked at from the far left-field, through a coloured prism. I make no apologies and there is no disclaimer. While I am clearly just the typist I'd still arm wrestle sailors for ribbons, anytime.

Salut, salut, Jx

The Author

Jenni Fagan is an author, poet, screenwriter, essayist and playwright. She has won awards from Creative Scotland, Arts Council England, Dewar Arts and Scottish Screen, among others, and was named one of the Best Young British Novelists by Granta in 2013, a once-in-a-decade accolade. Her debut novel, *The Panopticon*, was in Waterstones Eleven as one of the best worldwide debuts in 2012. Jenni has twice been nominated for the Pushcart Prize, was shortlisted for the Dublin Impac, Dundee International Book Prize, the Desmond Elliott Prize and the James Tait Black Prize, and has recently written for BBC Radio 4, *The New York Times*, the *Independent* and *Marie Claire*. Jenni lives in Edinburgh.

Note on the Type

The Dead Queen of Bohemia is set in Dante, a mid-twentieth-century book typeface designed by Giovanni Mardersteig, originally for use by the Officina Bodoni. The original type was cut by Charles Malin. The type is a serif face influenced by the types cut by Francesco Griffo between 1449 and 1516.